MY MOMMY'S IN THE MILITARY

Written by Kelly Caggiano-Hollyfield
Illustrated by Daniela Frongia

My Mommy's in the Military

Published by Publish Authority
300 Colonial Center Parkway, Suite 100
Roswell, GA 30076
www.PublishAuthority.com

MY MOMMY'S IN THE MILITARY
KELLY CAGGIANO-HOLLYFIELD

ISBN: 978-1-954000-64-3 (hardcover)
ISBN: 978-1-954000-65-0 (paperback)
ISBN: 978-1-954000-66-7 (ebook)

JUVENILE NONFICTION / Picture Books
JUVENILE NONFICTION / Parenting

Book Design by Michelle M. White

The views and opinions expressed in this book are those of the author.
They do not reflect the official position of the US Government,
Department of Defense, or the United States Space Force.

QUANTITY PURCHASES:
Schools, companies, professional groups, clubs, and other organizations
may qualify for special terms when ordering quantities of this title.
For information, email orders@publishauthority.com.

Publish Authority

To Jason, Lily, Mom, and Dad for supporting me on this journey.

To Matthew for inspiring me with the idea for the story.

And to my fellow moms in the military
to help tell your story to your own children.

Hi! My name is Matthew.

My friends and I are part of a special group of kids just like you.

Our mommies are in the military!
They do all sorts of jobs.

My mom works in Cyber Operations.

She works with computers
to protect all of our
cyber networks.

Networks are like invisible
highways that help us
share important
information.

My mom is an Engineer. She helps design, build, and repair things like ships!

Or planes! Or buildings!

The military needs special equipment to do a lot of different tasks, my mom makes sure everything is built exactly the right way.

Our mom is a Boom Operator.

She flies in the back of a big airplane and controls a long arm called a boom.

She uses the boom to put gas in other planes while both planes are flying!

My mom is a Veterinarian.

The military has specially trained animals, like dogs, that help with important missions.

My mom keeps the animals healthy.

My mom works in Logistics.

She helps get important equipment to other military members or people in need all around the world.

Sometimes she loads it on a plane, sometimes on a ship, sometimes a train, or she may just load it on a truck and drive it where it is needed!

My mom works in Special Operations.

She goes on unique missions.

She needs extra training before she can go.

Our mom is a Judge Advocate, that's a military Lawyer!

She makes sure that other military members obey the law.

Military law is called the Uniform Code of Military Justice, or UCMJ.

Our mom works in Communications.

She makes sure important information about the military is explained to civilians (that's people who are not in the military).

She's sort of like a journalist, but for the military instead of a newspaper.

My mom works in Space Operations. She operates satellites in space.

These satellites are objects that circle, or orbit, the Earth.

Some can take pictures, some provide navigation, or some even get weather information from around the world!

She's also part of the newest military branch called the Space Force.

Sometimes our moms deploy — that means they have to go away for a long time and usually to a different country.

Sometimes our moms work long days or nights, so we don't get to see them much, even when they are home.

But no matter where our moms are, or what they are doing, they are keeping us safe.

Other people may call them Soldiers, Sailors, Marines, Airmen, Guardians, or Coast Guardsmen, but we just call them Mom!

About the Illustrator

Daniela Frongia, known as Caisarts, a Sardinian-born digital illustrator, started her journey at 5. After Art School, she moved to London, specializing in various art forms.

Her digital flexibility enables work from anywhere, focusing on children's book illustration, covers, and character design.

She collaborated with authors and animation studios and featured in magazines, including "Be Artist" in 2019 and 2022.

About the Author

Kelly Caggiano-Hollyfield is an officer in the United States Space Force. She began her military career operating satellites in the United States Air Force and transferred to the Space Force in 2021. She has deployed to Afghanistan in support of Operation FREEDOM'S SENTINEL and Operation RESOLUTE SUPPORT. She is the proud mom to a 3-year-old son and 12-year-old daughter. A New Jersey girl born and raised, she is currently stationed in Virginia with her husband, children, and two cats.

Printed in the USA
CPSIA information can be obtained
at www.ICGtesting.com
LVHW061156070224
771186LV00018B/415